A TEACHER'S GUIDE TO THE MYSTERY OF THE COINS

by Chaya M. Burstein

UAHC Press
New York

Copyright © 1988 by
The UAHC Press
Manufactured in the United States of America
1 2 3 4 5 6 7 8 9 0

CONTENTS

Introduction 1
Using "The Mystery of the Coins" 2
Meeting the UAHC Curriculum Guidelines 3
Detailed Lesson Plans for the Introduction
and Chapters 1, 2, and 3
    Introduction—Uncle Otto's Trunk 6
    Chapter 1—The Golden-Headed Horse 8
    Chapter 2—Trouble at the Temple 11
    Chapter 3—Joseph the Carver 14
Lesson Plan Suggestions for Chapters 4-17
and the Conclusion
    Chapter 4—The Cave 20
    Chapter 5—A Fair Trade 22
    Chapter 6—The Rememberer 24
    Chapter 7—Pepper Pot's Pidyon Haben 26
    Chapter 8—The Double Purim 28
    Chapter 9—The Messenger and the Monkey 30
    Chapter 10—Even God Has to Be Fair 32
    Chapter 11—Asa and the Stranger 34
    Chapter 12—Goodbye, Golem 36
    Chapter 13—Moussa Ibn Dayan Helps Out 38
    Chapter 14—The Egg and Potato Passover 40
    Chapter 15—Shmulik, Srulik, and Itzik 42
    Chapter 16—Honor Your Father 44
    Chapter 17—Kaddish 46
    Conclusion 48
Source Materials 49
Student Handouts
    I   Timeline . . . . Center
    II Map of the Story Locations 54
    III Building a House of Jewish Law 55
    IV Holiday Symbols Scramble 56
    V   Nineteen Galut Lands 57

INTRODUCTION

If a modern Jewish child and a child from one of the wandering tribes of Israel met, what would they say to each other? What could they have in common? One child might talk about computers, youth-group dances, and video tapes; the other might tell of herding sheep, dancing at a campfire, and hauling water from a well. The differences would be unbridgeable—except in one area. Both are children of the covenant between God and the Jewish people, sharing a code of ethics based on the Torah and the Ten Commandments; identifying with the Land of Israel as a Jewish homeland and the Hebrew language as the language of the Torah, shared by all Jews; and feeling a kinship with other Jews.

As the centuries roll on, the differences between the children begin to shrink. A nomadic people, later a nation of farmers living in the Land of Israel, becomes a people scattered around the world, living largely in cities. Prayer and study in synagogues replaces the priesthood and the pomp and sacrifice at the ark and in the Temple. The Talmud and later writings interpret the Torah, helping the people adapt to new conditions. But the earliest, most basic links continue to be important: God, ethics, Torah study, Hebrew language, and identification with Israel and with other Jews.

The stories in this book establish a physical link between the centuries which illustrates the cultural-religious link. Two children and their grandmother find a collection of centuries-old coins. In tracing the origin of these coins, they evoke stories which tell of the problems, pleasures, and adventures of Jewish children over a period of 130 generations. The readers will find the differences between their own lives and the lives of the people in the stories dramatic, but the similarities such as prayer, holiday observance, and community responsibility are even more dramatic. Concepts of Jewish identity, historic continuity, prayer and faith in God, and ethical imperatives are personalized and dramatized for modern children as they peek through this window into the lives of their peers over the centuries.

USING "THE MYSTERY OF THE COINS"

The short-story format which rapidly spans the centuries is intended to give the reader a view, in perspective, of the incredible, dramatic journey of the Jewish people. This can later be supplemented by more detailed study in a conventional textbook.

The seventeen stories and the Introduction may be the basis of a year's work in a once-a-week history session at a part-time religious school. At least two sessions would be required for each story. In the first session historical background would be provided, the story would be located on Student Handouts I and II (timeline and map), unfamiliar words would be explained, and the introduction to the story would be read. The second session would include discussion of the story and activities related to it.

A day school with more frequent classes could cover the material in greater depth. Suggestions in the lesson plans and in the UAHC William and Frances Schuster Curriculum guide, *To See the World through Jewish Eyes: Guidelines for the Intermediate Years*, can be used to extend each chapter to three or four sessions.

The stories may also be used as enrichment material rather than as text if read in conjunction with study in a history textbook.

For home use these stories will be entertaining reading and will serve as informal education.

For classroom use the teacher should prepare the following teaching aids:
1. A large map of Europe and the Mediterranean world.
2. A line to be hung across the room to serve as a "mobile" timeline.
3. Clothespins or clips for fastening objects to the line.
4. Oversized models of the objects and coins illustrated at the beginning of each chapter. One of these will be hung on the timeline during the discussion of each story. Objects prepared by the students will be hung with each coin model. (See Chapter 1, first-session activities 3 and 4.)

MEETING THE UAHC CURRICULUM GUIDELINES

The Mystery of the Coins can be used to implement the objectives described in the UAHC William and Frances Schuster Curriculum guide, *To See the World through Jewish Eyes: Guidelines for the Intermediate Years*. Activities in the UAHC curriculum which are indicated in the chart below can be added to those listed in this guide.

Chapters in the Mystery of the Coins

UAHC Objectives/Activities	1	2	3	4	5	6	7	8	9	10	11	12	13	14	15	16	17	concl.
I Developing Jewish Functional Skills	10	18a b d	14		16	1 21	1 15a						15d		5a	5a	↑	
II Perspectives on Self and Others	11 8b 12c		12c			5e 22e		20	20	12 13 22b	19c	19	18 22d	17e 19a	12 20c	18c,g,h 20b,c 3a,b	↑	19 20 3a
III Gaining Jewish Insights	3a 17c 17a 19a,b	8a,b 17c 17a	3a 17c		3a		12a,b		12b						5a			
IV Continuity and Change	8 4 2 11b	8a,b	8a	6					6b							3	↑ ↑ ↑	8a 4e 8d 4
V Creative Thinking, Experience, and Expression	8				5		6a,b					1				2e 3a,b	↑	

**DETAILED LESSON PLANS
FOR THE
INTRODUCTION AND CHAPTERS 1, 2, and 3**

Introduction
UNCLE OTTO'S TRUNK

Synopsis

A mysterious coin collection is found in an old trunk. The last words of the owner of the trunk had been, "It's blood money! Give it back!" Jamie, Sarah, and Grandmother begin to identify the coins, hoping that the coin descriptions will give a clue to their ownership. They soon realize that the collection spans Jewish history. As each coin is identified, it tells a story—not to Jamie, Sarah, and Grandma, but to the reader.

Goals of the Lesson
1. To introduce the main characters and the theme of the book: Jewish history as it was lived by Jewish boys and girls throughout the centuries.
2. To examine coins and recognize them as clues to history.

Lesson Plan

Motivation:

Ask the students: If you had a time machine that could take you into any part of Jewish history, where would you want to go? Would you want to stay and live in that place and time? Since we have no time machine we will travel into history with the help of coins. In our travels we may find a favorite century or country. First let's see what coins tell us about history.

Activities:
1. Students should study coins from their pockets, noting such findings as date, place, language, and national symbol. List these on the board.
2. Have students study two or three coin illustrations in the book. Findings may include the religion of the ruling power (a cross or a crescent), the historic person or event being commemorated, the place and date that the coin was struck, the technological level of the coinmaker. Add these to the list.
3. Read the introductory chapter aloud with the class.
4. Explain to the class the use of a timeline to keep the coins in chronological order. Distribute Student Handout I and stretch a timeline clothesline across the room.
5. Ask the students: What is a timeline? Answers should in-

clude: a line drawn on paper or another surface to show past events in the order in which they happened. The class should discuss the meaning of B.C.E. and C.E. The explanation should include: Historic time in the Western World is divided into two periods, (1) the years before the birth of Jesus, before the Common Era (B.C.E.) and (2) the Common Era (C.E.). Students should practice counting backwards on their timelines for B.C.E. and forward for C.E. They should count backwards to 1400 B.C.E. and write Moses in the first box, then count forward to 1988 and write Jamie, Sarah, and Grandma in the last box.

6. Ask the class: Does Jewish history start with Moses? What is the first story in the Bible? Why do you think this story of Jewish history starts with Moses? Answers should include: Until the Exodus the Jews were a tribe or a group of tribes rather than a people. The journey in the desert, the receiving of the Torah, and the conquest of the Land of Israel unified the tribes into a nation.

Conclusion:

Point out that the book will tell about Jewish boys and girls throughout history. Ask whether the students in the class would have anything in common with them. If yes, what? Answers may include: the Hebrew language, the Torah and other books of religion, connection to the Land of Israel, and holidays. Have the class discuss this again at the end of the book.

Suggested Activities with Parents

1. Examine together foreign coins brought home from trips.
2. Visit the numismatic section of a museum.
3. Draw a timeline of the family's life starting with the birth of the student, the parents' wedding, or even earlier.

Bibliography

Adult:

Coins Reveal. Samuel and Daniel M. Friedenberg collection of coins and medals, Vol. 1. New York: Jewish Museum, 1983.

Frank, Harry T., ed. *Atlas of the Bible Lands.* Nashville, Tennessee: Broadman, 1979.

Roth, Cecil. *A Short History of the Jewish People.* New York: East and West Library, Hebrew Publishing Co., 1978.

Chapter 1
THE GOLDEN-HEADED HORSE

Synopsis

Rafi is encamped before Mount Sinai with his frightened parents and his older brother Binyamin, whom he greatly admires. With the help of Moses, Rafi proves that he can face the desert and its dangers as bravely as his brother.

Goals of the Lesson

1. To help the students relate to the fear and uncertainty of the Hebrews on leaving Egypt and facing the dangers of the desert.
2. To show the growth of self-confidence along with a growing belief in God and in the leadership of Moses.

Lesson Plan (first session)

Motivation:

With the students, read the introduction to Chapter 1 aloud. Present such clues as matzah, a seder plate, a toy snake, a wooden staff, etc., and ask the students to guess how these objects relate to the story they will read. Students should guess which holiday falls into the time period that Grandma described.

Activities:

1. Students tell the story of Passover, of slavery in Egypt, and of the Exodus. Add historical background including the arrival of Jacob's family in Egypt, the growth in the number of Hebrews, their enslavement, and Moses' campaign to free them.
2. Begin a vocabulary list on the bulletin board. Review B.C.E. and C.E. and explain the meaning of "tell," a hill or mound made of layers of ancient towns, each town built on the ruins of the earlier ones.
3. Have students cut out and tape the Golden-Headed Horse in place on their timelines. Introduce a box of large coin symbols to be hung on the clothesline timeline. Have one student find the horse symbol and clip it in place.
4. Explain that the clothesline will also serve as a timeline of Jewish customs. As the students find familiar customs, holidays, or objects mentioned in the stories they may bring in a drawing or model of the object or custom and hang it beside the appropriate coin.

5. Assign the story of "The Golden-Headed Horse" for home reading, or begin to read it in class.

Lesson Plan (second session)

Motivation:

Have students retell the story. Remind them that the Haggadah tells each of us to feel personally freed from slavery in Egypt. Keeping the story in mind, have the class reconstruct the feelings of the Israelites.

Activities:

1. What did Rafi and his parents feel in the desert? Make two lists, one of good feelings and one of bad feelings. Answers might include: anger at being dragged away from "safety" in Egypt, fear of the desert's dangers such as wild animals and snakes, hunger, thirst, loneliness, enemy tribes. Positive answers might include: the joy of being free to worship God, the joy at their release from forced labor, the excitement at the opportunity to return to the Land of Israel, their gratitude and respect for Moses.

2. Ask the students how they would feel if they were in Rafi's and Binyamin's place.

3. If space and noise are not problems, play a game of "Follow Moses" (Follow the Leader). With the help of the class, set up an obstacle course of chairs and tables (mountains), rope snakes, threatened ambushes, etc. Discuss the class reactions afterwards.

4. Rafi learned an important lesson from Moses. It was restated by Rabbi Hillel many years later: "In a place where there are no adults (competent people), strive to be an adult." How did that apply to Rafi? The answer should indicate that he was able to help his brother when the older boys had given up.

5. Ask the class: Does Hillel's statement have meaning for us? Have the class give examples. Possible examples include: helping with younger siblings or preparing a meal when a parent is ill, taking on a big job with a team or club because there's nobody else who will do it.

6. If additional class sessions are planned, further activity can include reading the Bible (Exodus 19 and 20:1-7) to find out what happened next to Rafi and the other Israelites. The class may also go into the synagogue sanctuary to look at the symbolic Ten Commandments above the ark or at the Torah scroll unrolled to the Ten Commandments.

Conclusion:
>Ask what Jewish object or custom the students found in the story which is still in use today. Students may draw or make a model for the timeline and bring it to the next class. Summarize the discussion on the mixed fear and joy that the Israelites felt on entering the desert. When else might this have happened in history or in a student's personal life? Answers might include: the feelings of the Puritans on the Mayflower; the feelings of Jews emigrating from Europe to the United States; a student's feeling at moving from a small, restrictive grade school to a large, challenging junior high school.

Suggested Activities with Parents
1. Waste basket archeology can help explain what archeologists learn from tells. Empty a wastepaper basket onto newspaper (add soda cans, broken pens, etc., if necessary) and see what you can learn of the life and culture of the owner.
2. Sleep in a tent in the backyard or in your sukah. Go camping. Discuss how it must have felt to be in the dark, empty desert.

Bibliography
>*Adult:*
>>"Exodus." *Keeping Posted,* Vol. XXXII, No. 5, March 1987. New York: Union of American Hebrew Congregations (UAHC).
>>Roth, Cecil. *A Short History of the Jewish People,* pp. 3-11.

Chapter 2
TROUBLE AT THE TEMPLE

Synopsis

At Sukot, Sarah, the shepherd girl, comes to the Temple in the great, crowded city of Jerusalem. Her parents come to worship and to arrange a marriage for her. But Sarah, who plays the flute, wants only to hear the music of the Levites, the Temple musicians. Before the pilgrimage ends, Sarah's music heals a terrified farmer but endangers the fine match her parents have arranged.

Goals of the Lesson

1. To make a transition from the nomadic, tribal life of Moses' time to the village life at the time of the early monarchy.
2. To describe the great pilgrimage holidays when Jews came to the Temple in Jerusalem, relating them to contemporary celebrations.

Lesson Plan (first session)

Motivation:

With the class, review the story of "The Golden-Headed Horse." Hang on the clothesline the Jewish objects that the students have prepared. Have a student read aloud the introduction to "Trouble at the Temple." Note that neither the horse nor the bracelet is a coin. They precede the development of coins. Is there a similarity between the societies in which they were used? Look at some pictures with the class to help decide.

Activities:

1. Using *Daily Life in Bible Times*, show pictures of nomads in the desert. Then show scenes of Solomon's Temple and the city of Jerusalem. Students should discuss the differences they've noted in the life style. These may include: house vs. tent; settled artisans, herders, and farmers vs. herders; peoplehood vs. tribal ties.

2. However, life remained simple. As an example, describe making pita bread by stretching dough over hot rocks. The pita serves as the fork and the spoon and the rock serves as the oven. Then distribute pieces of pita for the class to taste.

3. Give a brief historic background to serve as transition be-

tween Chapters 1 and 2. Describe the conquest and settling of Canaan, the period of Judges, and the beginning of the monarchy.

4. One student should hang the bit of bracelet on the clothesline timeline. Students should tape the bracelet on their own timelines.

5. Assign "Trouble at the Temple" to be read at home, or begin reading it in class.

Lesson Plan (second session)

Motivation:

Have students retell the story. Ask why Sarah and her family went to the Temple. Can the students explain the meaning of the words "Shalosh Regalim" or of the word "pilgrimage"?

Activities:

1. With the class, define "Shalosh Regalim" as the three pilgrimage holidays—Sukot, Shavuot, and Pesach—when Jews came to worship and bring sacrifices to God at the Temple. Add the term to the vocabulary list.

2. Have the students describe the holiday celebration as reported in the story. Discuss how Sukot is celebrated today. Is there music in the synagogue? If not, why not?

3. Show pictures of digs around the Temple Mount today, then ask the class: What is the Kotel, the Wall, or the Wailing Wall? Add "Kotel" to the vocabulary list.

4. Invite a parent or other person who has visited Jerusalem and has slides of the Temple area to show them to the class. Invite a parent or student who plays the flute or recorder to play for the class.

5. Tape a large sheet of mural paper or brown wrapping paper (about 32" x 60") on the wall and draw on it a large representation of the Temple. Have the students draw, color, and cut out pilgrims, priests, soldiers, animals, booths, jugglers, etc., and tape them in place on the Temple walls and courtyards.

Conclusion:

Ask the class to list those things in the story that are still part of Jewish life today. Are things described which Jews no longer do? Answers might include: animal sacrifice, matchmaking, pilgrimage, priesthood.

Suggested Activities with Parents:
1. Build a model of the Temple. (See *A Kid's Catalog of Israel*.)
2. Look up the story of young David who played music to ease the sadness of King Saul. In the Bible, read I Samuel 15:12-17.
3. Build a model sukah.

Bibliography

Adult:

Daily Life in Bible Times. Washington, D.C.: National Geographic Society, 1967.

"The Harvest Festivals." *Keeping Posted,* Vol. XXX, No. 2, November 1984.

Roth, Cecil. *A Short History of the Jewish People,* pp. 13-23.

Schauss, Hayyim. *The Jewish Festivals*. New York: UAHC, 1938.

Student:

Burstein, Chaya M. *A Kid's Catalog of Israel*. Philadelphia: Jewish Publication Society (JPS), 1988.

Drucker, Malka. *Sukkot: A Time to Rejoice*. New York: Holiday House, 1982.

Kuskin, Karla. *Jerusalem, Shining Still*. New York: Harper and Row, 1987.

Chapter 3
JOSEPH THE CARVER

Synopsis

At the age of fourteen Joseph is already a master stonecarver in Babylonia. When King Cyrus permits the exiled Jews to return to the Land of Israel, Joseph must decide whether to give up his work and privileges and go back with his family to a hard, dangerous life or to remain in exile.

Goals of the Lesson

1. To tell of the exile of the Jews to Babylonia and their return to Judea.

2. To demonstrate the toughness and flexibility of the exiles in holding to their religious beliefs while adapting those beliefs and practices to meet the new conditions of life in Babylonia.

Lesson Plan (first session)

Motivation:

With the class, review the story of "Trouble at the Temple." Hang on the clothesline the Jewish objects which the students have prepared. Point out that Chapters 1 and 2 have told about moving from place to place, walking through the Sinai Desert, and walking to the Temple. This story, "Joseph the Carver," is about a difficult and tragic move which might have caused the end of the Jewish people. Before reading the story with the class, discuss moving and how it affects people.

Activities:

1. Ask the students: Have any of you moved here from another neighborhood? How did you feel before you moved? Frightened? Hopeful? Ask the students how they would feel about moving. What things would be most important to take to a new home? What personal qualities would be most helpful in adjusting? Answers should include: a thick skin, friendliness, self-confidence, and faith in God and family.

2. Have the students assess the advantages and disadvantages of moving. Possible disadvantages: leaving behind such important things as a pet, garden, or one's own room; no friends; not knowing locations of stores, library, etc.; difficulty of getting used to a new school, new teacher, or new classmates. Possible advantages: new, more interesting friends; a better school; better

facilities such as a team, pool, or club in the new neighborhood.

3. Play the game, "I'm moving to Babylonia and I'm taking along a _____." Each student should repeat the phrase in turn, adding a personal choice to the items chosen by previous students, e.g., "I'm moving to Babylonia and I'm taking along a Bible, a water jug, a camel...." As the list grows students will forget words and drop out. The best "rememberers" remain.

4. Continue the historical background. At first, Babylonia was a very sad place for the Jews. The people missed their homes, and they missed the great Temple. Why was it so important? Answers should include: the security of being in God's house under God's protection, sacrifices, holiday festivities, music. Because they wanted very much to keep living as Jews they began to create substitutes. The substitute for the Temple still serves us today. What is it? (The synagogue.) The priests didn't lead prayers in the synagogue. Who did? (Rabbis and teachers.) Forty years after the Jews had settled into their towns and jobs, a new king conquered Babylonia. To all the conquered people who had been brought to Babylonia, he gave permission to return home. Some Jews were thrilled, some were not. In the story of "Joseph the Carver," we'll discover how one 14-year-old boy felt about returning, and what he did.

5. Have a student read aloud the introduction to the story. Students should then tape the gold stater in the correct place on their timelines and clip the large stater on the clothesline.

6. Explain the unfamiliar words which appear in the story: Marduk—a Babylonian deity; street shrine—a booth on the street where priests of the gods accepted offerings and said prayers for the donors; Judea—part of the original Land of Israel which included Jerusalem (the northern part of the Land of Israel had been conquered and lost long before). Add "galut," the Hebrew word for exile, to the vocabulary list. All the places where Jews have lived outside of Israel have been called "galut."

7. Distribute Student Handout II for the class to do.

8. Assign "Joseph the Carver" for home reading, or begin to read it in class.

Lesson Plan (second session)

Motivation:

Have students retell the story. Remind the class of the advantages and disadvantages of moving from place to place. Were there also advantages and disadvantages for the Jews in being taken from Judea into "galut," exile?

Activities:

1. Students should list positive and negative aspects of Galut Bavel (the Babylonian Exile). Negatives should include the loss of the beloved Temple and the Temple ceremonials, the loss of homes and family members, the loss of freedom and pride, a sense that God had abandoned the people. Positives should include: a growing strength and determination to remain Jews even outside the Land of Israel, the development of substitutes for the Temple and the priests in the form of synagogues, Torah study, and rabbis.

2. Point out that some Jews including Joseph's parents were eager to return to Judea while others were unwilling. Draw a parallel to 1948 when the State of Israel was established. Many Jews from all over the world returned to Israel at that time, and some are still returning. Ask the students if they know of people who went. Family? Friends? Ask the members of the class how they would feel if, like Joseph, they were asked to return.

3. Going to live in Israel is called "aliyah," Hebrew for "going up." Add aliyah to the vocabulary list.

4. Sum up the history which followed the return. Unlike Joseph and his family most of the Jews of Babylonia did not go on aliyah to Judea. They continued to live and worship and study in exile. Many years later, after another terrible war in Judea, Jews escaped to Babylonia and found refuge with their kin. Point out that the class will read more about this in Chapter 7.

Conclusion:

Comment that a time of war and exile is a tragic time in people's lives. The Babylonian Exile has been called the "dress rehearsal" for all the exiles to come in Jewish life. What does this term mean?

Suggested Activities with Parents

1. Find the story of the Tower of Babel in the library or read

the Bible, Genesis 11:1-9. The English word babble derives from Babylonia which was the site of the Tower of Babel. The tower may have been a ziggurat, a stepped tower with a shrine at the top. The Temple of Marduk was probably also a ziggurat.

2. Modern Iraq and Iran occupy the lands of ancient Babylonia. These countries are often in the news. Clip out articles to discuss or bring in to class.

Bibliography

Adult:

Raphael, Chaim. *The Road from Babylon*, pp. 19-26. Jerusalem: Steimatzky.

Roth, Cecil. *A Short History of the Jewish People,* pp. 46-54.

Student:

Garfield, Leon. *King Nimrod's Tower.* New York: Lothrop, Lee, and Shepard Co.

LESSON PLAN SUGGESTIONS
FOR
CHAPTERS 4-17 AND THE CONCLUSION

For Chapters 4-17 and the Conclusion, in addition to the suggestions in the lesson plans that follow, each lesson should include: reading the chapter introduction aloud; taping the timeline symbol on Student Handout I; hanging the large coin symbol on the clothesline timeline; hanging symbols of customs and objects on the clothesline timeline; and adding words to the vocabulary list.

Chapter 4
THE CAVE

Synopsis

Two close friends, Hayyim and Meir, share a secret hideout in a cave near their Judean village. As their families are caught up in the conflict between Hellenistic and Pharisaic Jews, the boys are forced apart. They meet in the cave for a last time to save endangered villagers from the Syrian-Greeks.

Goals of the Lesson

1. To describe the background of the revolt of the Maccabees against the Syrian-Greeks.
2. To show the conflicts of Greek culture and coercion within the Jewish community.

Suggested Class Activities

1. Describe Greek cultural influence in Judea, e.g., in philosophy, art, architecture, sports, and idolatry. While it was most attractive to the city dwellers and the upper classes, it was resisted by the villagers.
2. Have the class retell the Chanukah story. Discuss the effectiveness of guerrilla warfare. The patriots of the American Revolution were guerrillas. Do you know of guerrilla fighters today?
3. Choose a "Meir" and a "Hayyim" from among the students to debate the virtues of Hellenism versus Judaism.
4. To illustrate a basic tenet of Judaism that is very different from the intolerant Hellenism of Antiochus, read "Hillel and the Stranger" in "Source Materials" at the end of this guide.
5. Ask the students to bring in their family's Chanukiah (Chanukah menorah). Discuss the meanings of the decorative symbols. Since Chapter 4 tells of both faith and battle, have the students draw shields for Maccabee fighters and decorate them with symbols to represent Judaism or the fight against Hellenism. Display them on a wall of the classroom.

Suggested Activities with Parents

1. Museum trip to see sculptures of Greek gods and pictures on vases which give clues to Greek life.

2. Jewish museum trip to see the wide variety of historic Chanukah menorot.

Bibliography

Adult:

Fast, Howard. *My Glorious Brothers.* New York: Hebrew Publishing Co., 1977.

"Roots of Chanukah." *Keeping Posted,* Vol. XXII, No. 3, December 1976.

Roth, Cecil. *A Short History of the Jewish People,* pp. 64-76.

Student:

Chaikin, Miriam. *Light Another Candle: The Story and Meaning of Chanukah.* New York: Clarion Books, 1981.

Chapter 5
A FAIR TRADE

Synopsis

The Holy Temple is destroyed, and Judea is conquered by the Romans. Judean prisoners and loot from the Temple are paraded before the horrified eyes of Esther and her family, who are Roman Jews. Esther's sadness at losing her Jewish homeland is eased when she finds a way to save a tiny Judean prisoner.

Goals of the Lesson
1. To show the transition of Jews from a people centered in Judea to groups dispersed in the galut, in exile.
2. To show continuing ties to the Land of Judea/Israel and to fellow Jews wherever they may be.

Suggested Class Activities
1. Describe expanding Jewish settlement throughout the Greek and Roman empires. After the revolt against Rome, many more Jews of Judea were forcibly scattered abroad.
2. Show photo of the Arch of Titus, still standing in Rome, and identify the pictured Temple treasures. (See *Wanderings*.)
3. Ask the class how Jews kept the memory of the Temple alive. (Torah study, folktales, Tishah Be'av, casting dough, breaking the glass at a wedding.)
4. Explain pikuach nefesh. Is this still a Jewish concern? How? Have the class plan a personal expression, e.g., writing to a Refusenik family.
5. Discuss Esther's feelings as a Jew and a Roman. Did she have divided loyalty? Do American Jews?
6. Have the students think of possible conflicts such as deciding whether to root for an Israeli soccer team that is competing with an American team, an Israeli tennis player against an American, or the much more serious question of how to relate to the Pollard spy affair. Have the students prepare a skit to illustrate the conflict and their feelings about it.

Suggested Activity with Parents

To remember Jerusalem, make a mizrach hanging for the

eastern wall of the house.

Bibliography

Adult:

Potok, Chaim. *Wanderings,* pp. 220-221. New York: Knopf, 1978.

Roth, Cecil. *A Short History of the Jewish People,* pp. 96-108.

"The War against Rome." *Keeping Posted,* Vol. XXVI, No. 6, March 1981.

Chapter 6
THE REMEMBERER

Synopsis

Rivka loved to hear Savta Nehama tell stories about the teachings of the wise rabbis of Israel. She listened closely and remembered every word. When her grandmother died, she was very lonely until she found that she could feel close to her grandmother by continuing her job of relaying the wisdom of the past to the scribes who were writing it all down in the Mishnah.

Goals of the Lesson

1. To describe the continuing, strong Jewish life in Judea under Roman rule.
2. To explain the reasons for codification into the Mishnah of the verbal rulings of the rabbis.

Suggested Class Activities

1. Describe life in Judea after the revolt. Jews concentrated on spiritual survival rather than on political rebellion.
2. Explain the difference between Torah shebichetav (written Torah—the Bible) and Torah shebe'al peh (oral Torah—the commentaries on the Bible which were remembered and retold from generation to generation). Why did the rabbis begin to write down Torah shebe'al peh?
3. What is meant by the Talmud's words, "make a fence around the Torah"? Play a circular fence game. Place a person called "Shabbat" in the center. Think of Shabbat rules or customs, e.g., chalah, candles, no work or travel, etc. For each rule, add another circle of students around Shabbat. Have some students try to break in to "harm" Shabbat. The more rules, the more circles, the more protection.
4. Rememberers have always provided historic knowledge. Ask the students if there are rememberers in their families who recall the depression, the Second World War, the Holocaust, and/or the birth of Israel. Interview them and tape their stories for the class.

Suggested Activities with Parents

1. Activity 4, above, is a good family project.

2. In the synagogue library, look at a volume of the Talmud. Note the section of Mishnah in the center, surrounded by commentaries.

Bibliography

Adult:

"The Mishnah." *Keeping Posted,* Vol. XX, No. 4, January 1975.

Roth, Cecil. *A Short History of the Jewish People,* pp. 114-118, 124-128.

Student:

Pomerantz, Barbara. *Bubby, Me, and Memories.* New York: UAHC, 1983.

Spero, Moshe Halevi. *Zeydeh.* Simcha Books, 1984.

Chapter 7
PEPPER POT'S PIDYON HABEN

Synopsis

Penina misses her favorite uncle who has become a Karaite Jew. He believes that Penina and her family are breaking Torah laws, and he refuses to visit them. When Penina's nephew is born, she begs her uncle to come and help with the pidyon haben. But his "help" makes a bad situation even worse.

Goals of the Lesson

1. To show Judaism's continuing adaptation to changing environments and the resulting internal conflicts (Rabbanism vs. Karaism).
2. To introduce Islam, a new factor in Jewish life, which was to become as important as Christianity.

Suggested Class Activities

1. Describe the increasing persecution of Jews in Palestine when the Roman rulers became Christian. Jews began to leave. Many went to Babylonia where Jews had self-rule and great academies of Torah study.
2. Describe Islam, the religion of Babylonia. It is called a daughter religion of Judaism (one God; no pork; day of rest; the Islamic bible, the Koran, based on the Torah).
3. Show the photographs of Arab-Islamic life that appear in the *National Geographic* magazine. Name some modern Islamic countries.
4. Tell of the conflict between Rabbanite and Karaite Jews. If Karaism had won, how would our lives be different today? Read aloud "The Oral Law" in "Source Materials" at the end of this guide. How does this story apply to Rabbanites and Karaites? Does it apply to Jewish life today?
5. Have any students who have attended a pidyon haben tell what happened. The words mean "redeeming the son." Redeeming from what?

Suggested Activity with Parents

Visit the rabbi of a synagogue to discuss how the synagogue handles disagreements on Shabbat observance, kashrut, etc.

Bibliography
Adult:
Roth, Cecil. *A Short History of the Jewish People,* pp. 128-133, 149-156.

"Saudi Arabia." *National Geographic* magazine, June 1966.

Stillman, Norman A. *The Jews of Arab Lands: A History and Source Book.* Philadelphia: JPS, 1979.

STUDENT HANDOUT I
Timeline

Timeline boxes (starting from START HERE, going around):

B.C.E. (descending): 1400, 1300, 1200, 1100, 1000, 900, 800, 700, 600, 500, 400, 300, 200, 100 B.C.E.

C.E. (ascending): 1 C.E., 100, 200, 300, 400, 500, 600, 700, 800, 900, 1000, 1100, 1200, 1300, 1400, 1500

B.C.E.
- **1400s** Hebrews leave Egypt and enter Israel.
- **1300s** Judges rule Israel.
- **1100s**
- **1000s** Monarchy begins. Temple is built.
- **900s** Kingdom splits into two.
- **900s–600s** Prophets write and teach.
- **700s** Northern Kingdom is destroyed.
- **500s** Temple and Southern Kingdom are destroyed, Jews are exiled and return.
- **300s** Greeks conquer Judea.
- **100s** Maccabees revolt.

C.E.
- **100s** Revolt against Rome. Temple is destroyed. Christianity begins.
- **200s** Rabbis write the Mishnah.
- **200s–500s** Babylonian center grows.
- **500s** Rabbis write the Talmud.
- **600s** Islam begins.
- **900s** Golden Age in Spain begins.
- **1100s–1300s** Crusaders hit Jewish communities.
- **1400s** Jews expelled from Spain.
- **1600s** False messiahs. Jews come to the New World.

↑ START HERE

C.E.

1700s Chasidism grows.
1800s Equal rights are granted to Jews in Western Europe. Reform movement begins.
1900s Zionist movement grows. Mass Jewish migration from Eastern Europe to the U.S.
1940s Holocaust in Europe.

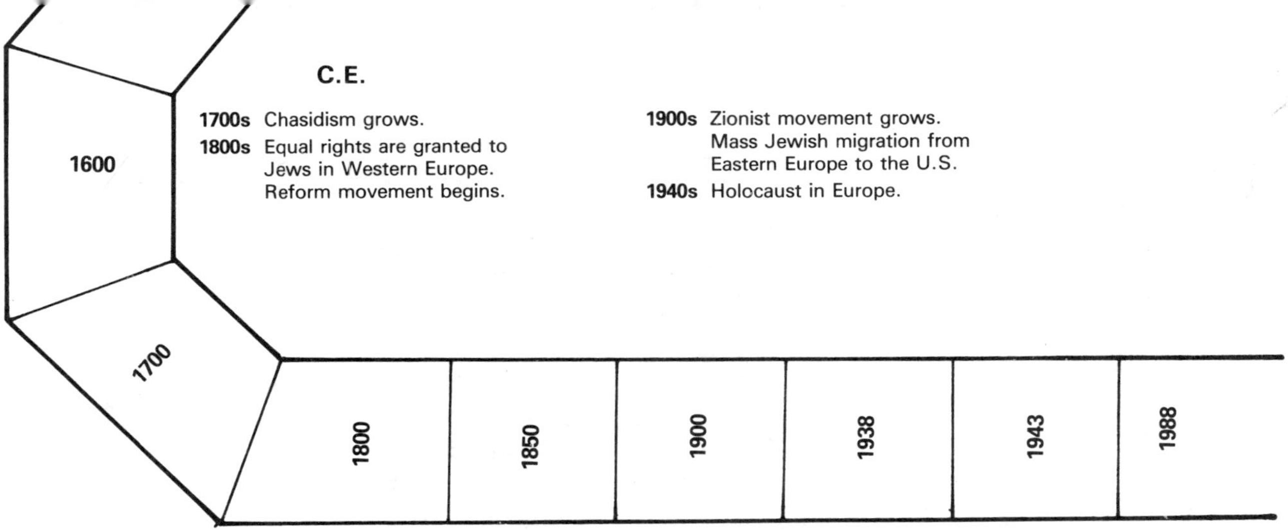

1600 | 1700 | 1800 | 1850 | 1900 | 1938 | 1943 | 1988

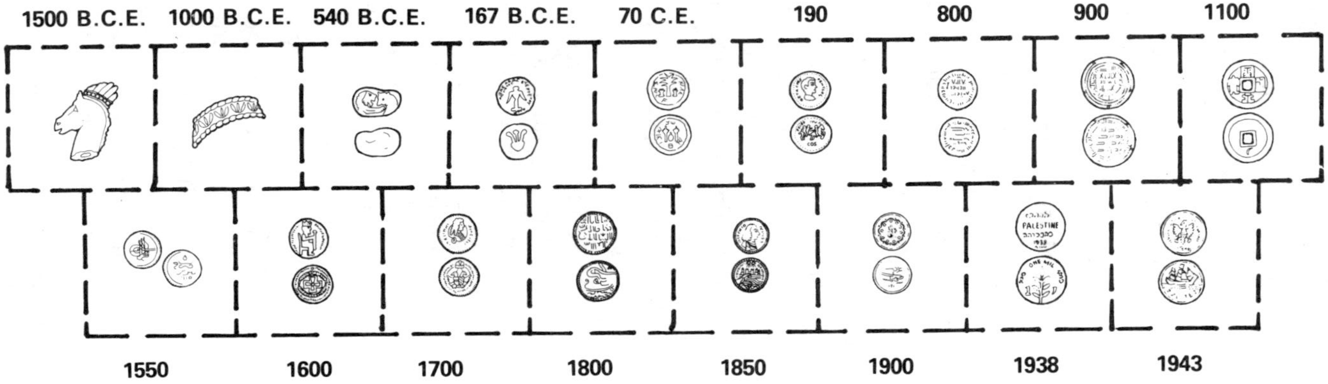

1500 B.C.E. | 1000 B.C.E. | 540 B.C.E. | 167 B.C.E. | 70 C.E. | 190 | 800 | 900 | 1100

1550 | 1600 | 1700 | 1800 | 1850 | 1900 | 1938 | 1943

Chapter 8
THE DOUBLE PURIM

Synopsis

Arieh's father, a Babylonian physician, is called away from a Purim feast to attend to the caliph of Cordova. If he fails to heal the caliph, he will be put to death, and the Jews of Cordova will be endangered. Arieh, who serves as his father's apprentice, is burned by hot oil when a rival physician tips the oil lamp that Arieh is holding. But Arieh steadies the lamp and saves the day.

Goals of the Lesson
1. To show the shift of the Jewish religious and cultural center from Babylonia to Spain.
2. To show the vulnerability of Jews even in tolerant Muslim Spain.

Suggested Class Activities
1. Describe the decline of Babylonia and the shift of Jewish population and cultural centers to Spain. How were Jews able to move with comparative ease from Babylonia to Spain? (Coreligionists who lived in Spain and shared language and family ties were ready to help; many Jews [e.g., doctors, scholars, merchants] had "moveable" skills.)
2. Today, do American Jews help Jews from other lands? How? (United Jewish Appeal, Joint Distribution Committee, political action for Russian Jewry, etc.)
3. Describe the Golden Age of Spain. Explain the special Jewish contributions which served as a bridge between the East and the West. Tell about Judah Ha-Levi, Abraham ibn Ezra, etc. Read the poems by ibn Gabirol and Ha-Levi in the "Source Materials" at the end of this guide.
4. According to a Yiddish proverb, "There are so many Hamans but only one Purim." Tell the Purim story. Have the class make comic masks of such other "Hamans" in Jewish life as Hitler, Pharaoh, and Antiochus. Draw a gallows on a large sheet hung on the wall. Tape the masks as though hanging from the gallows or use the masks to play a game of "Pin the Nose on Haman."

Suggested Activity with Parents

Make funny Purim masks or puppets of the caliph, Arieh,

and the storyteller.

Bibliography
Adult:
Raphael, Chaim. *The Road from Babylon,* pp. 67-113.
Roth, Cecil. *A Short History of the Jewish People,* pp. 171-175, 194-199.

Student:
Greene, Jacqueline Denbar. *Butchers and Bakers, Rabbis and Kings.* Silver Spring, Maryland: Kar-Ben, 1984.

Chapter 9
THE MESSENGER AND THE MONKEY

Synopsis

Abraham is waiting on the dock in Aden for an Egyptian ship. The Jewish captain of the ship is bringing a responsa message from the great Rabbi Mosheh ben Maimon—a message that may endanger the whole Jewish community if it falls into the hands of the governor. The captain arrives and is arrested, but Abraham manages to save the responsa.

Goal of the Lesson

To describe two major unifying factors for Jews of diverse lands: the Hebrew language and the law of the Torah, as interpreted by wise rabbis and communicated through responsa.

Suggested Class Activities

1. Describe the Jews of Yemen and Aden who may have moved south after the destruction of Solomon's Temple. Show pictures of Yemenite Jews (*The Vanished Worlds of Jewry*, pp. 162-171).

2. The Egyptian captain spoke to Abraham in Hebrew. What language would you share with a Jew from a faraway country? Choose two students to be Abraham and the captain. Have them speak to each other in Hebrew and/or in sign language; have the class help with such phrases as shalom, le'hitra'ot, boker tov, etc. Does the class know other "international" Jewish languages? (Yiddish, Ladino.)

3. What are responsa? Why did Jews need them? (Not many communities had copies of the Talmud to consult, and there arose such new problems as Karaism and false messiahs.)

4. Have the class make up some responsa questions of the future. (Can I allow my robot to clean the house on Shabbat or must it rest? When shall I celebrate the holidays while traveling through space in a time warp?)

5. Distribute Student Handout III for the class to do.

Suggested Activity with Parents

Look through Leo Rosten's *The Joys of Yiddish*. Pick out Yiddish words that have become part of the English language.

Bibliography

Adult:

"Maimonides." *Keeping Posted,* Vol. XXXI, No. 1, October, 1985.

Patai, Raphael. *The Vanished Worlds of Jewry.* New York: Macmillan, 1980.

Rosten, Leo. *The Joys of Yiddish.* New York: McGraw-Hill, 1968.

Roth, Cecil. *A Short History of the Jewish People,* pp. 178-181.

"Travels of Benjamin of Tudela." *Keeping Posted,* Vol. XXI, No. 8, May 1976.

Chapter 10
EVEN GOD HAS TO BE FAIR

Synopsis

The winter rains haven't fallen on Safed in northern Israel although Grazia and her family have prayed and used amulets and magic formulas to call for God's help. When Grazia's mother decides to slaughter the baby goats to save water, Grazia becomes very angry. She scolds God for being so cruel and runs away with her goat. Then a torrent of rain pours down, leaving her frightened, drenched, but happy.

Goals of the Lesson

1. To give a brief description of the expulsion of the Jews from Spain in 1492 and to describe the Zionism that brought some of the exiles to the Land of Israel.
2. To describe some superstitions and folktales that became part of Jewish culture and daily life.

Suggested Class Activities

1. Tell the class the story of the expulsion from Spain and the dispersion of the Jews throughout the Mediterranean world, including Safed, Palestine.
2. Safed was a great Jewish center of study. The Kabbalah and the Shabbat song "Lechah Dodi" were written in Safed. It was also a center of superstitious lore. How is a superstition different from a religious custom? Is a mezuzah superstition? Is a hamsa (a hand, a Sephardic Jewish symbol)? What superstitions do many people have today?
3. Grazia's father said the rain had not come "because our sins are great." Ask the class: When bad things happen are they God's punishment for our sins?
4. Was it wrong of Grazia to scold God? To show the tradition of exchange of views between God and the Jews, read aloud "Kaddish" by the chasidic Rabbi Levi Yitzhok of Berditchev in "Source Materials" at the end of this guide.

Suggested Activity with Parents

Read together some of the folktales listed in the bibliography.

Bibliography

Adult:
Roth, Cecil. *A Short History of the Jewish People,* pp.

236-252, 279-286.

"A Story-Telling People: Folk Tales and Folklore." *Keeping Posted,* Vol. XX, No. 1, October 1974.

Student:

Roseman, Kenneth. *The Cardinal's Snuff Box.* New York: UAHC, 1982.

Schwartz, Howard. *Elijah's Violin: And Other Jewish Fairy Tales.* New York: Harper and Row, 1983.

Chapter 11
ASA AND THE STRANGER

Synopsis

Asa and his family live high in the mountains of Ethiopia and work as blacksmiths. When Asa goes down to the hostile Christian village, he feels weak and alone. He thinks that he and his relatives are the only Jews left in the world. One day, a strange, pink-faced trader appears in the village. He saves Asa from a beating and recognizes him as a fellow Jew. "We're not alone!" Asa joyously rushes to tell his parents.

Goals of the Lesson
1. To point out that Jews have belonged to varied races and nationalities.
2. To discuss the problems of being part of a small group living amidst a much larger group.

Suggested Class Activities
1. Give a brief history of the Jews of Ethiopia and show pictures from *Keeping Posted*.
2. Discuss what groups there are in Judaism. Then, show pictures from *The Vanished Worlds of Jewry* and/or from *All in My Jewish Family*.
3. What's a minority? What's a majority? Is it a problem to be part of a minority? Never? Always? At holiday time? Discuss how to deal with the problem. Prepare a skit to illustrate the problem.
4. Ethiopian Jews kept many Jewish customs for centuries. To demonstrate how hard this can be, teach a simple Hebrew song in a round or sing "Row, Row, Row Your Boat." Have one or two students sing one part while the majority sings the other part.
5. Give examples of name-calling, racist terms, or "Polish" jokes. Why are they used? Are they harmful? Why?

Activity with Parents

Read together parts of *There's No Such Thing as a Chanukah Bush, Sandy Goldstein*. Then discuss the family's holiday observances.

Bibliography
Adult:
"The Falashas." *Keeping Posted,* Vol. XXVI, No. 5,

February 1981.

Patai, Raphael. *The Vanished Worlds of Jewry.*

Rapoport, Louis. *The Lost Jews.* Briarcliff Manor, New York: Stein and Day, 1980.

Student:

Roseman, Kenneth. *All in My Jewish Family.* New York: UAHC, 1984.

Sussman, Susan. *There's No Such Thing as a Chanukah Bush, Sandy Goldstein.* Racine, Wisconsin: Whitman, 1983.

Chapter 12
GOODBYE, GOLEM

Synopsis

Shloimy loved animals and games, but he hated studying. He was also so stubborn that he couldn't turn down a dare. When his friend challenged him to climb to the attic of the Altneu Synagogue to find the golem, Shloimy accepted. He grew more and more frightened as he climbed. But at the top he found only a talit and a pile of gray dust. Shloimy used the talit to rescue a trapped bird and therefore lost the bet, but he didn't care. He'd made the right choice.

Goals of the Lesson

1. To discuss mitzvot (commandments and/or good deeds) in Jewish tradition.

2. To describe aspects of Jewish life in central Europe: ghetto, study, synagogue, etc.

Suggested Class Activities

1. Tell the story of the golem or read aloud "The Mechanical Man of Prague" in *Let's Steal the Moon* or "The Golem" in *Keeping Posted*.

2. Discuss the meaning of "ghetto" and "blood libel." How did the ghetto walls affect Jewish life? Are there still ghettos today? (Ghettos of the Holocaust, ethnic ghettos in the large cities.)

3. Shloimy's father thought Torah study was a very important mitzvah. Make a list of other important mitzvot (tza'ar ba'alei chayim, compassion for living things; tzedakah, charity, responsibility for fellow Jews; etc.).

4. Tell or read the legend of Altneushul in "Source Materials" at the end of this guide, which shows the traditional link with Israel and its history.

Suggested Activities with Parents

1. Discuss ways to improve the care that the family gives its pets.

2. Make and illustrate a chart of other mitzvot the family may carry out.

Bibliography
Adult:
Altshuler, David. *The Precious Legacy: Judaic Treasures*

from the Czechoslovak State Collections. New York: Summit Books, 1984.

"The Golem and Other Fairy Tales." *Keeping Posted,* Vol. XXIX, No. 3, January 1984.

Student:

Burstein, Chaya M. *Joseph and Anna's Time Capsule: A Legacy from Old Prague.* New York: Summit Books, 1984.

Ish-Kishor, Shulamith. *A Boy of Old Prague.* New York: Pantheon, 1963.

Serwer, Blanche Luria. *Let's Steal the Moon.* New York: Little, Brown, 1970.

Stadtler, Bea. *The Adventures of Gluckel of Hameln.* New York: United Synagogue Book Service, 1967.

Chapter 13
MOUSSA IBN DAYAN HELPS OUT

Synopsis

Ruhama is soon to be married, and she is frightened. She doesn't know who her husband will be, or where they will live. Accompanied by her younger sister, Naima, Ruhama makes a risky trip to the tomb of a holy man and prays for a good husband. In the next few days, it is Naima's turn to be miserable. There will be boys only, five younger brothers, in the house after Ruhama marries. But Ruhama tells Naima a secret at the wedding: the holy man promised a new baby sister for Naima as well as a good husband for Ruhama.

Goal of the Lesson

To describe and compare the two major groups of Jews: the Sephardim and the Ashkenazim.

Suggested Class Activities

1. Compare the previous story which tells of European (Ashkenazic) Jews in a Christian land with this story of North African (Sephardic) Jews in a Muslim land. Write the names Shloimy and Naima on the board. Under each, list differences (daily language, Yiddish vs. Judeo-Arabic; clothing; prayer ritual) and similarities (Torah and Talmud; synagogue and rabbi; ghetto).

2. There are many differences between Ashkenazic and Sephardic foods, even between Ashkenazic and Sephardic Passover foods. Divide the class into two groups. Have one group prepare an Ashkenazic charoset, and the other a Sephardic charoset. (See *A First Jewish Holiday Cookbook,* or find charoset recipes in other Jewish cookbooks.)

3. Ask the students if they have ever been to a Jewish wedding. How do they think Ruhama's wedding would be different? How would it be the same?

Suggested Activities with Parents

1. Look at the family photo album and talk about your parents' wedding. What was especially Jewish about it?

2. Discuss the family name and the family's origin to decide whether it is Sephardic or Ashkenazic.

Bibliography

Adult:

"Jews of Arab Lands." *Keeping Posted,* Vol. XXII, No. 4, January 1977.

Patai, Raphael. *The Vanished Worlds of Jewry,* pp. 100-115.

Student:

Burstein, Chaya M. *A First Jewish Holiday Cookbook,* p. 74. New York: Bonim Books/Hebrew Publishing Co., 1979.

Chapter 14
THE EGG AND POTATO PASSOVER

Synopsis

In a blinding snowstorm on Passover eve, Isaac and his peddler father are reluctantly given shelter in a barn on a Pennsylvania farm. The farmer and his family are drawn to the "Israelites" by curiosity and by their shared love of the Bible. The lonely seder eve becomes a friendly, happy time of learning about each other.

Goals of the Lesson
1. To tell of early Jewish immigration to the United States.
2. To describe the mixture of interest and fear that some Christians and Jews felt toward each other.

Suggested Class Activities
1. Tell of early immigration to the United States: first Sephardic, then Ashkenazic.
2. What work did Isaac's father do? Why did many Jewish immigrants become peddlers? Relate to the class such famous success stories as those of Macy's and Gimbel's.
3. Why was the farmer so familiar with the Bible? (Both Christians and Muslims see the Bible as their holy book, and some study it in addition to their own Christian Scriptures and Koran.)
4. Who was the prophet Elijah? What part does he take in the Passover seder? Teach the song "Eliyahu Hanavi" and/or read *The Magician* aloud. Ask the class: Can you think of a time when you would have wanted Elijah's help?
5. Distribute Student Handout IV for the class to do.

Suggested Activities with Parents
1. Visit a Jewish museum to see some miniature Jewish ritual objects carried by merchants in their travels. Identify other ritual objects in the home or synagogue. Discuss what they are for, where they are made, etc.
2. Discuss the work your family's first American ancestors did. Where did they live?

Bibliography
Adult:
Birmingham, Stephen. *Our Crowd.* New York: Berkley

Books, 1985.

"A Century of German Jewish Immigration." *Keeping Posted,* Vol. XXIII, No. 2, October 1977.

Student:

Burstein, Chaya M. *The Jewish Kid's Catalog,* pp. 50-55. Philadelphia: JPS, 1984.

Meltzer, Milton. *Taking Root: Jewish Immigrants in America.* New York: Farrar, Straus and Giroux, 1976.

Shulevitz, Uri. *The Magician: An Adaptation from the Yiddish of I.L. Peretz.* New York: Macmillan, 1978.

Chapter 15
SHMULIK, SRULIK, AND ITZIK

Synopsis

Shmulik, Srulik, and Itzik were best friends who did everything together. One day, when a pogrom broke out in their small Russian town, they were able to end it by setting fire to the home of the leader of the pogrom. Instead of being happy at their success, the boys were sad. They realized that they must leave Russia and leave each other to build new homes in friendlier lands.

Goals of the Lesson

1. To describe the lives of Jews in Eastern Europe.

2. To show the beginning of the mass migration to Western lands.

Suggested Class Activities

1. In the 1800s, a majority of the world's Jews lived in Eastern Europe. Describe small-town Jewish life in Eastern Europe. Play part of a recording of the musical play *Fiddler on the Roof* and/or read aloud from *Life Is with People*.

2. Were Shmulik, Srulik, and Itzik right to set the fire? What would you have done to stop the pogrom? Read the talmudic quotes that appear in the "Source Materials" at the end of this guide. Discuss them with the class.

3. On leaving the shtetl where would you have gone? Choose three students to represent Shmulik, Srulik, and Itzik and have them debate their choices. Include later events such as the Holocaust and the establishment of the State of Israel in considering the choices.

4. Discuss names. Shmulik, Srulik, and Itzik, which are really Shmuel, Yisrael, and Isaac, became Sam, Yisrael, and Otto. What are the Hebrew names of the students in the class? When must Hebrew names be used? (At all Jewish religious events.)

Suggested Activities with Parents

1. In the New York City area, go to the immigration museum in the base of the Statue of Liberty and to the Lower East Side.

2. Practice writing your Hebrew name and the names of

your parents and siblings. If you are named after a relative, find out whatever you can about that person. Write a biography of the relative.

3. Make a Hebrew nameplate for your door.

Bibliography

Adult:

Roth, Cecil. *A Short History of the Jewish People,* pp. 356-359, 387-393.

Samuel, Maurice. *The World of Sholom Aleichem.* New York: Knopf, 1943.

"What's in a Name?" *Keeping Posted,* Vol. XVIII, No. 1, October 1972.

Zborowski, Mark, and Herzog, Elizabeth. *Life Is with People: The Culture of the Shtetl.* New York: Schocken Books, 1962.

Student:

Burstein, Chaya M. *Rivka Bangs the Teakettle.* New York: Harcourt Brace Jovanovich, 1970.

_____. *Rifka Grows Up.* New York: Bonim Books/Hebrew Publishing Co., 1976.

Rabinovich, Shalom (Sholom Aleichem), Shevrin, Aliza, trans. *Holiday Tales of Sholom Aleichem.* New York: Scribner's, 1979.

Chapter 16
HONOR YOUR FATHER

Synopsis

Lisa disobeys her father who wants her to escape the Nazis by going to England. She joins a group of boys and girls who are making their way illegally to the shores of Palestine. She almost drowns when their small ship is chased by a British warship and runs aground off the coast.

Goals of the Lesson

1. To describe briefly the history of Palestine in the nineteenth and twentieth centuries.
2. To describe the dangers of escaping from Europe and reaching Palestine in the years before the establishment of the State of Israel.

Suggested Class Activities

1. Ask the class who ruled Palestine when Srulik got there. (Turks.) Describe the change after the First World War when Great Britain became the mandatory power and many new Arab states were established. Great Britain set increasingly tight immigration quotas for Jews, which resulted in illegal immigration.

2. Poet Robert Frost said that "home is a place where, when you want to go there, they have to let you in." Did Jews have a place they could call home before the State of Israel was founded?

3. If space and noise are not problems, divide the class into the British and immigrant Jews and play a variation of "Red Rover."

4. Divide the class into groups of no more than ten for an Aliyah Race Quiz. Tape up a chart on which you have drawn a track for each group. Draw a large box at the end. Mark it Palestine. Divide the track into about eight boxes. Tape a ship in the first box at the beginning of each track. Ask quiz questions alternately, moving a ship ahead one box with each correct answer until the winning group reaches Palestine. See the diagram and suggested questions for the quiz in "Source Materials" at the end of this guide.

Suggested Activity with Parents

Play the "Going Up" game, available from Alternatives in Religious Education, or "The Aliyah Game" in *Aliyah: One*

Step at a Time, available from the UAHC Department of Education.

Bibliography
Adult:
> Kimche, Jon, and Kimche, David. *The Secret Roads: The Illegal Migration of a People.* Westport, Connecticut: Hyperion Conn, 1976. Reprint of 1954 ed.

Student:
> *Aliyah: One Step at a Time.* New York: UAHC Department of Education, 1987.
>
> Burstein, Chaya M. *A Kid's Catalog of Israel.*
>
> Eisenberg, Azriel, and Ain-Globe, Leah, eds. *Home at Last.* New York: Bloch, 1976.
>
> *"Going Up": The Aliyah Game.* Alternatives in Religious Education, Inc., 3945 S. Oneida St., Denver, Colorado 80237.
>
> Kluger, Ruth, and Mann, Peggy. *The Secret Ship.* New York: Doubleday, 1978.

Chapter 17
KADDISH

Synopsis

Berelleh escapes the massacre in which his parents, sister, and other villagers are killed by the Nazis. He lives in the forest with a group of partisans, feeling alone and wishing that he too were dead. Then he joins the Jewish fighters in the Warsaw Ghetto and has a brief moment of joy and revenge.

Goals of the Lesson

1. To give students a sense of the immensity of loss of life in the Holocaust.
2. To describe the resistance struggle of the Jews against Nazism.

Suggested Class Activities

1. Describe the rise of anti-Semitism and Nazism in Germany. What other stories in this book describe anti-Semitism? How was Nazism different?
2. Describe the loss of life in terms that the students can understand, e.g., a football stadium holds 60,000 people, 100 times that number died in the Holocaust. Divide the class into groups of six each to represent the world's Jewish population in 1939. Two students in each group would have been killed.
3. A million and a half children were also killed. Read together *The Children We Remember* or *I Never Saw Another Butterfly*.
4. What does the "Kaddish" mean? When is it recited? Why was it such an important prayer to Berelleh and his mother?

Suggested Activity with Parents

Are there relatives or friends that your family lost in the Holocaust? Find a way to remember them. Plant a tree in your garden, or contribute to the Jewish National Fund so that a tree may be planted in Israel.

Bibliography

Adult:

"Aspects of the Holocaust." *Keeping Posted,* Vol. XXI, No. 5, February 1976.

Dawidowicz, Lucy. *The War Against the Jews: 1933-1945.*

New York: Holt, Rinehart & Winston, 1975.

Roth, Cecil. *A Short History of the Jewish People,* pp. 422-444.

Student:

Byer, Chana Abells. *The Children We Remember.* Silver Spring, Maryland: Kar-Ben, 1983.

Ginsburg, Marvell. *The Tattooed Torah.* New York: UAHC, 1983.

Roseman, Kenneth. *Escape from the Holocaust.* New York: UAHC, 1985.

Stadtler, Bea. *The Holocaust: A History of Courage and Resistance.* New York: Behrman House, 1975.

Volavkova, Hana, ed., Nemcova, Jeanne, trans. *I Never Saw Another Butterfly: Children's Drawings and Poems from Terezin Concentration Camp, 1942-1944.* New York: Schocken, 1978.

CONCLUSION

Goal of the Lesson
   Summing up.

Suggested Class Activities
1. Say to the class: We've read stories that tell about more than three thousand years of Jewish history. What ideas or things have we found that we share with Jews who lived during these centuries? Name them and point them out on the clothesline timeline. What things have changed very much in Jewish life over these centuries?

2. Of all the times you have read about, when and where would you most want to live? Why?

3. Distribute Student Handout V for the class to do.

SOURCE MATERIALS

For Chapter 4:
Hillel and the Stranger
A certain heathen came to Shammai and said to him:
"Convert me provided that you teach me the entire Torah
    while I stand on one foot."
Shammai drove him away with a measuring stick, which
    was in his hand.

He went to Hillel who said to him:
"What is hateful to you, do not do to your neighbor:
that is the entire Torah;
the rest is commentary;
go and learn it."

—Talmud
From *The Rest Is Commentary*

For Chapter 7:
The Oral Law
Once I was on a journey, and I came upon a man who went
    at me after the way of heretics.
Now, he accepted the Written Law, but not the Oral Law.
He said to me:
"The Written Law was given us from Mount Sinai;
the Oral Law was not given us from Mount Sinai."
I said to him:
"But were not both the Written and the Oral Law spoken by
    the Omnipresent?
Then what difference is there between the Written and the
    Oral Law? To what can this be compared?
To a king of flesh and blood who had two servants and loved
    them both with a perfect love;
and he gave them each a measure of wheat, and each a bundle
    of flax.
The wise servant, what did he do?
He took the flax and spun a cloth.
Then he took the wheat and made flour.
The flour he cleansed, and ground, and kneaded, and baked,
    and set on top of the table.
Then he spread the cloth over it and left it so until the king
    should come.
But the foolish servant did nothing at all.
After some days, the king returned from a journey and came
    into his house and said to them:

'My sons, bring me what I gave you.'
One servant showed the wheaten bread on the table with a cloth spread over it,
and the other servant showed the wheat still in the box, with a bundle of flax upon it.
Alas for his shame, alas for his disgrace!
Now, when the Holy One, blessed be He, gave the Torah to Israel,
He gave it only in the form of wheat, for us to extract flour from it,
and flax, to extract a garment."

—Seder Eliyahu Rabbah
From *The Rest Is Commentary*

For Chapter 8:
Poems

by Solomon ibn Gabirol

When all within is dark,
And old friends turn aside;
From them I turn to You
And find love in Your eyes.

When all within is dark,
And I my soul despise;
From me I turn to You
And find love in Your eyes.

When all Your face is dark,
And Your just angers rise;
From You I turn to You
And find love in Your eyes.

by Judah Ha-Levi

In the East, in the East is my heart,
And I live at the end of the West.
How shall I join in your feasting,
How shall I share in your jest,
How shall my offering be paid,
And my vows carried out,
While Zion pines in Edom's bonds,
And I am held in the Arab's bound!
All the beauties and treasures of Spain
Are worthless as dust in my eyes;
But the dust of the Lord's ruined house
As a treasure of beauty I prize.

From *A Treasury of Jewish Poetry*

For Chapter 10:
Kaddish
by Levi Yitzhok of Berditchev
    (Russia, 1740-1809)
Good morning to You, Almighty God.
I, Levi Yitzhok, son of Sarah of
    Berditchev,
Have come for a judgment against You,
On behalf of Your people Israel.
What do You want of Your people
    Israel?
Why do You afflict Your people Israel?
The slightest thing and You say,
    "Speak to the children of Israel."
The slightest thing and You turn to the
    children of Israel.
The slightest thing and You say, "Tell
    the children of Israel."
Our Father! There are so many nations
    in the world,
Persians, Babylonians, Edomites.
The Russians, what do they say?
That their emperor is emperor.
The Germans, what do they say?
That their empire is the empire.
And the English, what do they say?
That their empire is the empire.
And I, Levi Yitzhok, son of Sarah of
    Berditchev, say,
"Magnified and sanctified be His great
    name!"
And I, Levi Yitzhok, son of Sarah of
    Berditchev, say,
"From this spot I shall not stir.
I shall not stir from this spot.
There must be an end of this.
The exile must end!
Magnified and sanctified be His great
    name!"

                        —Translated from the Yiddish
                                by Joseph Leftwich
                    From *A Treasury of Jewish Poetry*

For Chapter 12:
A Legend
When the Great Temple in Jerusalem was burning, angels flew into the flames and snatched stones from the crumbling walls. They carried the stones over the earth, dropping them here and there. Wherever a stone fell, a synagogue was later built. Many stones fell in the city of Prague, but, before the Jews could use them to build a synagogue, the angels set a condition. They said, "You may use these stones on condition (in Hebrew, "al tneu") that, when the Great Temple in Jerusalem is to be rebuilt, you will return them." To remember their promise, the Jews named the synagogue the "Altneu" Synagogue.

For Chapter 15:
Talmudic Quotes
Rabbi Hillel said: "If I am not for myself, who will be for me? But, if I am *only for myself*, what kind of person am I?"

Someone came before Raba and said: "The chief of my town has ordered me to kill so and so. If not, he will have me killed." Raba said to him: "Let him kill you, but you must not kill. Do you think that your blood is redder than another person's? Perhaps his blood is redder than yours."

Ausubel, Nathan, and Ausubel, Marynn, eds. *A Treasury of Jewish Poetry.* New York: Crown, 1957.

Glatzer, Nahum H., ed. *The Rest Is Commentary.* Boston: Beacon Press, 1961.

For Chapter 16:
Aliyah Race Quiz

Some suggested quiz questions:
- What does "aliyah" mean?
- What year was the State of Israel established?
- Why did Lisa and her friends jump off the boat?
- Who was the first prime minister of the new State of Israel?
- What is a Zionist?
- What does "jude" mean?
- What is a Nazi?
- Where does the phrase "honor your father and mother" come from?
- What is a kibbutz?
- In which country is the city of Tel Aviv?
- What was the Mossad?
- What does the word "ha-tikva" mean?
- Why is Hatikva a special song?
- What languages were found on the Palestinian coin?
- What was the coin called?
- What does "shalom" mean?
- What is a "hora"?
- Which country held the mandate over Palestine before Israel was established?
- What did Jamie, Sarah, and Grandma have for dinner after they identified the Palestine coin?

(Student Handout I can be found between pages 27 and 28 of this guide.)

STUDENT HANDOUT II

Map of the Story Locations

Locate on the map:
1. Sinai Desert (in Egypt)
2. Judea (State of Israel)—
   for Stories 2 and 4
3. Babylonia (Iraq)—
   for Stories 3 and 7
4. Rome, Italy
5. Galilee (in Israel)
6. Cordova, Spain
7. Aden (Yemen)
8. Safed (in Israel)
9. Ethiopia
10. Prague, Czechoslovakia
11. Morocco
12. Pennsylvania, U.S.
13. Russia
14. Palestine (Israel)
15. Warsaw, Poland

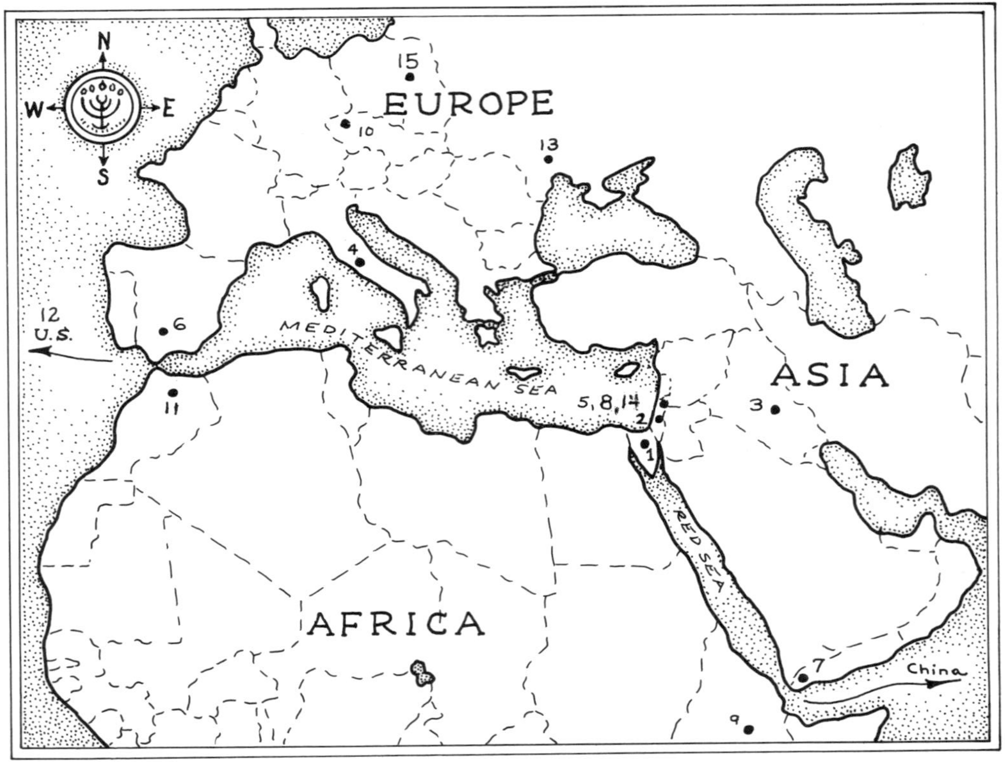

54

STUDENT HANDOUT III
Building a House of Jewish Law

Cut out the labeled building blocks. Tape them in the dotted line spaces. Start at the base with the earliest Jewish holy book.

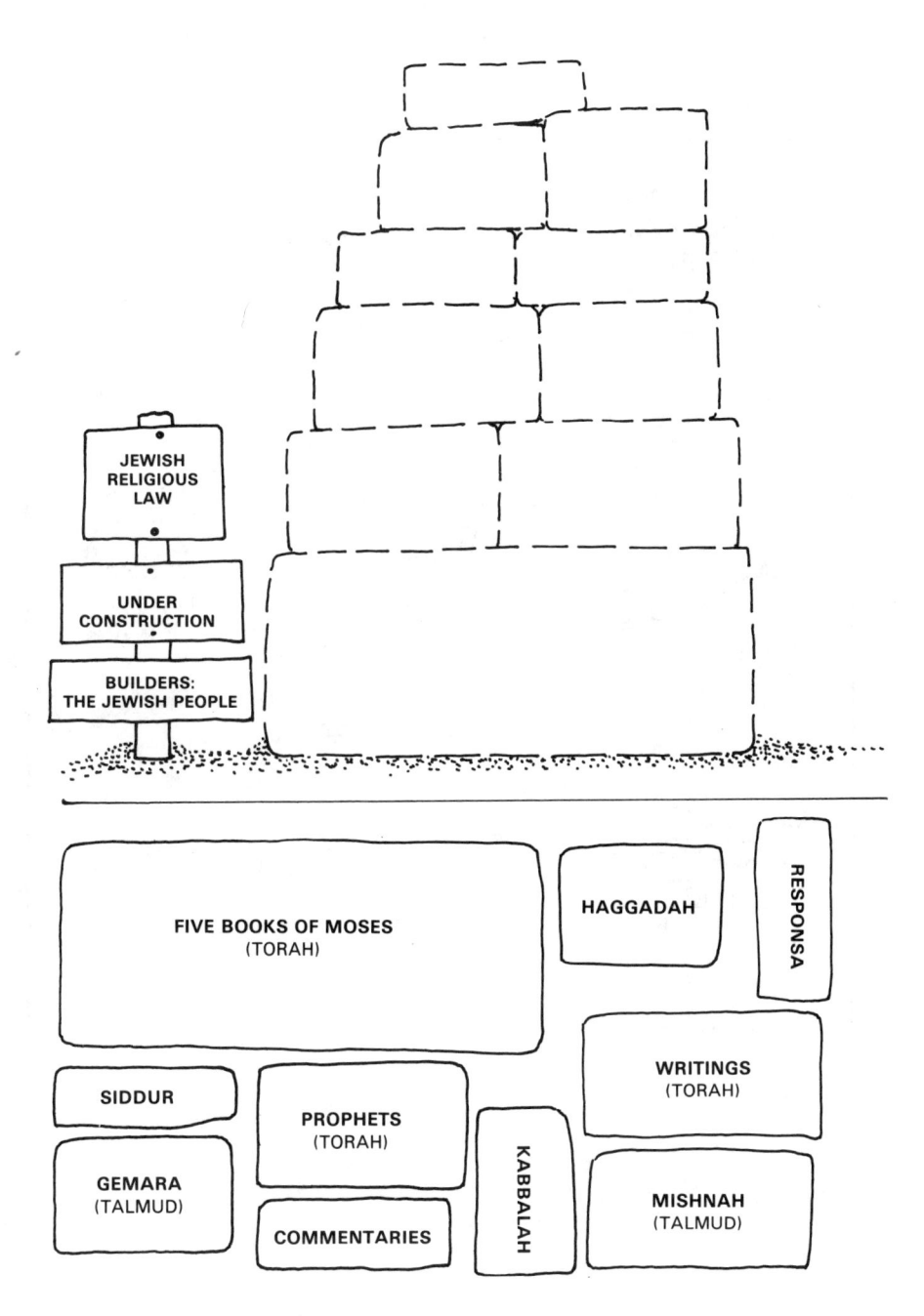

JEWISH RELIGIOUS LAW

UNDER CONSTRUCTION

BUILDERS: THE JEWISH PEOPLE

FIVE BOOKS OF MOSES (TORAH)

HAGGADAH

RESPONSA

SIDDUR

WRITINGS (TORAH)

PROPHETS (TORAH)

GEMARA (TALMUD)

KABBALAH

MISHNAH (TALMUD)

COMMENTARIES

STUDENT HANDOUT IV
Holiday Symbols Scramble

RANEMOH

HORSFA

DIDURS

LITLA

HAROT

HIPAK

EITFNLI

HEZZMUA

STUDENT HANDOUT V
Nineteen Galut Lands

P	I	Y	U	C	H	I	N	A
I	M	U	B	Z	O	L	O	M
P	O	T	Y	E	M	E	N	E
G	R	E	E	C	E	S	P	R
E	O	N	A	H	E	Y	O	I
R	C	E	P	O	A	R	L	C
M	C	R	U	S	S	I	A	A
A	O	O	R	L	F	A	N	E
N	A	M	B	O	R	E	D	T
Y	A	E	R	V	A	G	I	H
A	D	E	N	A	N	Y	N	I
I	R	A	N	K	C	P	D	O
S	I	N	A	I	E	T	I	P
F	O	S	P	A	I	N	A	I
B	A	B	Y	L	O	N	I	A

Babylonia Czechoslovakia Yemen
Ethiopia   Morocco   India
Russia   Egypt   Syria
Germany   Sinai   Iran
America   Poland   France
Spain   Aden
Rome   China